THE CATS
OF
SEA-CLIFF
CASTLE

by ETHEL JACOBSON / *photographs by* FLORENCE HARRISON

Ward Ritchie Press

To Mary George and Bob Parker, the best friends
a beach cat ever had.

Second Printing, 1973

Copyright 1972 by Ethel Jacobson
Library of Congress catalog card number 75-173235
ISBN 0378-60253-5
Printed in the United States of America
by Anderson, Ritchie & Simon, Los Angeles
Designed by Cas Duchow

Cats have lived for decades in a rocky cliff
on the southern California coast.
Over the years I have visited many generations of these cats, and
this story is based on that remarkable colony.
These photographs were made at the scene, and show
the present inhabitants at home.

ETHEL JACOBSON

The cliff
is a rambling castle.
It crowns the cove.

Weathered, deeply fissured, it has been carved
through patient centuries.
By California's chill winter rain and brilliant summer sun.
By storms that blow across the Pacific from far islands.
By wind and sand and sea spray.
Against the sky, its towers rear fanciful silhouettes.

At its base,
waves lap gently,
polishing worn pillars,
honing the scimitar of beach.
Rarely, a tempest churns
to fury, hurling mountainous
breakers against the shore.
Then the waters subside again,
smooth, shimmering, pacific.

The sea-cliff castle seems deserted.
But from a dozen vantage points, eyes look out.

From lofty parapets
they scan every approach.

From craggy bastions, ears prick the morning sky.
Below, the bay widens, merging with a sea that stretches
to the empty horizon.
Beyond the cliff, the hill rises brown and bare.

Presently—the cats come out.

Tiger and tabby, tawny and black, ring-tailed and plumed.

They roam the rocks.

They comb the gullies and caverns.
They stalk through tangles of ice plant
and toyon and thorn.

Clambering on stone,
patrolling the beach,
Visiting the jetty to the north,
They prowl their seaside domain.

When they return to their courtyards,
they wash.
Archie washes.
Lucifer washes.
Everyone washes.

In secluded nooks, barricaded by giant blades of agave
edged with needle-sharp spines,
are the nurseries.
Here come Molly and Midge and Sylvie to curve themselves
around clumps of squirming kittens.

The babies are washed. And fed.
And washed again.
In a few weeks they scramble out to explore
a harsh but fascinating world.

The castle is terraced and tunneled,
honeycombed with hidden galleries and chambers,
with secret passages and exits.
Sylvie chose a deeply recessed hideaway for her family.

Molly picked a cozy hollow warmed by morning sun.
In padded nests ringed by bristling thorns,
babies roll, tumble, and wave their paws.

Last spring, Midge's kittens
were disturbed by
screeching, swarming boys.

This year she and Griselda
pooled their families,
sharing a well-concealed nest.
There, while one mother goes
about her affairs,
the other remains on guard.
The arrangement pleases
everyone . . .
especially the kittens.

Like a mother cat, the cliff curves itself round the thin
crescent of shore scooped by the sea.
The castle itself is a great stone cat,
dabbling its paws in the shallows.
Morning finds it glistening, damp as a newly-washed kitten.
But soon mists vanish. Skies brighten.
And everywhere cats lie purring in the sun.

On terraces and balconies, in the lee
of intricately sculptured walls,
friends gather to share
sea air and sun,
the day's news, the latest gossip.

Later they seek the shade.
Siesta time is an old California custom.

But always someone is watching
sea and hill and cloud.
If a cormorant flies over,
if a pelican lands on a driftwood perch,
if a surf fisherman heads for the jetty
with a full bait pail . . .   someone knows.
And as soon as one cat knows, they all know.

Cats first came to the sea-cliff castle many years ago.
A stray or two wandered down from the hill . . . or from a fishing
boat . . . or was abandoned.
They foraged through the scraggly brush.
They fought the rats along the jetty.
They moved into their private palace.

And here from time to time
came other cats . . .
homeless waifs
or adventurous souls
who welcomed the challenge
and freedom they found.

Romance blossomed. Kittens were born.
The hill people took some home as pets.
Age and mischance—and the wanderlust that brought
some cats to the castle originally—took others . . .
maintaining a rough population balance.

For more than a decade Old Rufus
was something of a patriarch.
A mighty hunter and dashing swain,
he challenged his rivals
and serenaded his ladies long after
such actions had become
nothing but gallant gestures.
One raw day, grizzled and dim-eyed,
he hobbled off . . .
and knew he would not return.

Since then, the closest thing to a leader has been
the magnificent Jasper. An even more formidable fighter,
his zeal for battle in war or love is happily still undimmed.

But this kingdom has no ruler, this castle has no king.
Its lords and ladies owe no allegiance,
cherishing independence as only cats,
since the dawn of time, have done.

Sylvie was born in the nursery where her own kittens now lie.
Against the silver of her fur, emerald eyes gleam
like crown jewels. But from her pink mouth comes a voice
like the scrape of a broken shell.

Andy is the current dandy. He has feline friends on the hill,
fat cats with whom he dines on unaccustomed delicacies
and howls in the better alleys. But a swinging
morning or two later he returns to spindrift and sea tang
and his bachelor apartment in a castle tower.

Jinny was found on the hill.
Someone had forced her head into
a tin can and fastened it about her
neck. She ran off . . . but luckily
she ran into help.
Rescuers felt that after her ordeal
she might prefer life
with her own kind.
The castle cats welcomed her . . .
especially Archie. Now she, too,
is busy with her kittens,
the nightmare past apparently forgotten.

Lucifer likes the jetty,
where he is known
as the fastest paw on the beach.
Anglers will pretend
to ignore their bait pails,
just to marvel at his dexterity.
Lucifer, of course,
understands that it is a game.
He always obliges by an elaborate
show of crouching, wiggling,
and tail-lashing
before the lightning pounce.

Other friends from the hill leave welcome treats.
The cats instantly recognize a distant figure or a voice
that has won their trust. They watch . . . and wait.

Every tidbit is sniffed out . . .

speared . . .

relished to the last sliver.

The castle cats live together
in curious amity.
They share common tasks—
to preserve the peace,
promote the general welfare,
and keep the vigil.

In sun and mist,
in rain and starshine,
they scan the hills,
the heavens,
the ever-changing sea . . .

The sea that turns from emerald to jade
or flames from copper to amber-gold, reflecting
a skyful of sunset.
The afterglow lingers briefly, then fades
to the ashes of dusk.

As day wanes, evening mists blow away.
The westerly wind freshens and may even send
water devils dancing over the waves.
Again, the scene seems deserted.

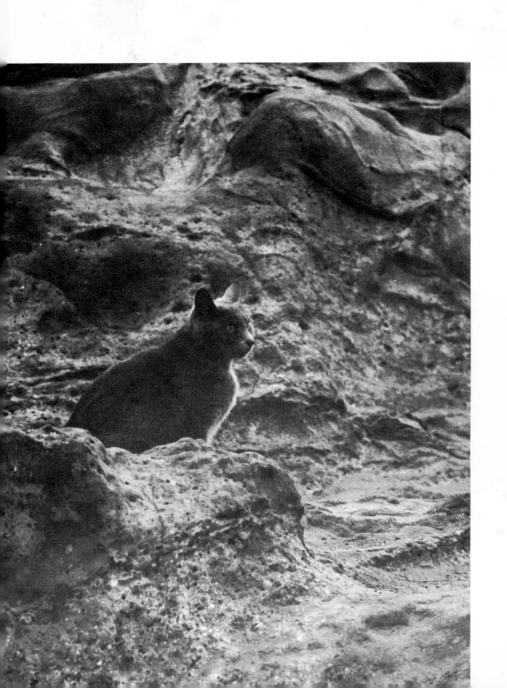

But the cats are there,
watching.
Kittens sleep safe
in their mothers' arms.

Soon the first stars
will blink in the sky.
Like cats' eyes.
Like the emerald
and jade
and copper and amber-gold eyes
that blink back
from shadowed ramparts.

Night falls
softly
on the rambling castle
that crowns the cove.